Veils *of* *Time*

Shadowed Veils of Memory

Betty Duncan-Goetz

Order this book online at www.trafford.com
or email orders@trafford.com

Most Trafford titles are also available at major online book retailers.

Printed in the United States of America.

ISBN: 978-1-4907-2141-5 (sc)
ISBN: 978-1-4907-2140-8 (hc)
ISBN: 978-1-4907-2139-2 (e)

Library of Congress Control Number: 2013922573

Trafford rev. 02/21/2014

 www.trafford.com

North America & international
toll-free: 1 888 232 4444 (USA & Canada)
fax: 812 355 4082

CONTENTS

CHAPTER 1

Shadowed Veils of Memory

THE SOFT, wispy veils float across my mind in colors of blue, green, white, and sometimes almost black. These gossamer waves, so unclear at times, then reveal memories as bright and crisp as though they happened yesterday—veils of memory, hiding little patches of times gone by, veils we wish we could forget, veils we are glad to push aside, so we may see those times again. They reveal memories we cherish, loved ones long gone, but there they are, just through the veil, the veil of memories.

Late at night as Becka and Red lay in the large guest room bed, they talked quietly about the events of the day. It had been an especially happy one. Becka's parents had really enjoyed their fiftieth wedding anniversary. All five of their children and their children's families had attended. Every one at the gathering was in seemingly good health and spirits. There was singing, laughter, eating (lots of eating), visiting, and catching up on all the events of each family. It was the type of gathering that especially pleased everyone. Becka's parents, Ben and Liz, loved having all of their children present, seeing their many grandchildren, and making sure they were all fed. Liz prided herself on always having delicious food and plenty of it! Except for the incident, indeed the near tragedy of little Nancy, everything had turned out well.

During the late evening of the outdoor festivities, Ben and Liz's great chow dog, King, had repeatedly come to Ben, and then to Red, whining and looking concerned. However, both men had given him a bit of food and paid no more attention to the dog. Later, when it came time to gather things together and for Harry and family to leave, Mikki, Harry's wife, called for their little daughter, Peggy, and her friend Nancy, who had traveled with them to Kentucky for the anniversary celebration.

But Nancy couldn't be found. They looked everywhere around the house and yard, calling the child all the while. Red asked Ben if he had seen the dog in the last few minutes. Both men looked concerned, remembering how the dog had behaved earlier, and both started to run toward the woods behind the house, whistling for the dog and calling Nancy.

When they found Nancy, she was disheveled and disoriented. She couldn't remember anything that had happened. The scene around her looked as if a battle had taken place. There was blood on the ground, and a bloody jacket lay beside King. King was obviously hurt and bleeding profusely. He was badly wounded, and they could only imagine what might have happened. The other men, Henry, Johnny, and Harry, had arrived on the scene by this time and they quickly made carriers of their pants for the child and the dog.

Harry and Johnny carried little Nancy and Red, and Henry carried the dog. Tears were streaming down Red's face. "This dog probably saved little Nancy's life, and he may die before morning," he thought to himself. And that thought proved true. When they got Nancy and the dog to the house, they called the doctor, and Maggie called a Vet for King. Ben called the police.

The doctor came swiftly, as did the Vet. When the doctor arrived, he pronounced Nancy unhurt physically and aware. He said she had fainted and probably didn't know what had happened. He had looked her over carefully and decided not to cause her more trauma by sending her to hospital. The Vet checked King over and said his condition was grave and that the next few hours would tell his fate.

The police came and very quickly found the owner of the bloody and torn jacket. He was hiding in the woods near the creek. His right arm and hand were bloody, and his clothes were torn. The dog had put up a great fight, and the man had run when he heard the whistles and calls for the child. He claimed he had found the child and the dog in the woods and meant no harm to either of them. The police nevertheless took him into custody, where he was treated and placed in jail.

Red and Ben told the police about the dog trying to warn them earlier. It turned out the man had been lurking in the woods and had no good intentions on his mind. It was an incident none of them would forget. The next morning, the old dog passed away. He was treated as a real hero with all the neighbors coming to his "funeral."

Becka and Red delayed their return trip for a day or two, until all settled down. Nancy told Peggy's mother that "someone had put a cloth" over her face and that that was all she could remember. Indeed, the police found the chloroform-soaked cloth near where the dog and Nancy were found. They had treated the cloth as evidence.

Mikki decided to let Nancy alone with no more questions until they got her back home to Florida and her parents' home. It would be time enough then to review what had happened. Peggy told her parents that she and Nancy and King had been playing hide-and-seek in the woods near the house and when she couldn't find Nancy or the dog she "just thought they would come back soon." Harry reminded Peggy and Nancy that they must always remember to play where they could be seen by their parents or other adults. However, they did not dwell on scolding the girls. They had had enough trauma for one day.

It was the summer of 1962. World War II had ended in 1945, and the Korean Conflict had ended nine years earlier. John F. Kennedy was president, and there was an atmosphere of confidence and the anticipation of a bright future.

The World War II veterans, who had returned home, had resumed their lives, finishing school, finding jobs, and starting families. Although they had scars, both mentally and physically from their wartime trials, they put them behind and charged full speed into their lives.

Becka's brothers, twins Harry and Henry and older brother Will, had returned. Harry finished graduate school, and he and his family moved to Pensacola, Florida, where he became dean of a dental school. He authored several medical books about dentistry, doing the illustrations himself for each book. He enjoyed his work and his children. He and his wife, Mikki, had four children, three boys and a girl. When Harry talked about his wartime experiences, it was always with fun and humor. He related the more humorous aspects of his time in the military, talking little about the dangers and hardships. Their oldest son, Stephen, visited Becka in California when he was grown. He enjoyed Becka's home and seeing Southern California, and he and Becka enjoyed talking about Harry and family memories.

Becka's youngest brother, Henry, married his favorite girl, Helena, soon after he returned from combat. He had been in the worst part of the war, if indeed any part of the war could be called "good." He had landed on the beach battleground at Normandy on "D Day minus four" and had fought his way through France and Germany. He had endured the "Battle of the Bulge" and was involved in close combat in both France and Germany.

Henry had seen many of his best friends literally blown apart in battle, and he had survived in a muddy, icy foxhole during the Battle of the Bulge. The Allied bombs came so close to his foxhole that he was literally lifted out of the hole when the bombs exploded, falling back onto the wet muddy ground, not knowing if he was still "all there" or even if he had been lucky enough to survive at all. The noise of the bombs was so fierce that he felt his head would explode! Yet, he came home from these terrible experiences saying very little about them and resuming his life.

Henry, like his brothers, was determined to get on with the business of living—making a family, finding and keeping a good job, and building a good life. Although they did not speak of it, they were determined to "make the world a better place" and the experiences of the war justifiable so that the sacrifices of so many of their buddies and friends would not have been made in vain. These young men had a fierce love of their country and wanted desperately to be part of a bright future for their children and grandchildren. They were indeed a part of the "greatest generation," as Tom Brokaw wrote in his book of the same name.

As Becka and Red talked quietly that evening after the celebration, Red held Becka close. He, like the twins and many of his wartime buddies, talked little about their war experiences. His own wartime adventures had often been filled with extreme danger. He had been in three airplane crashes during his military years. One was in the South Pacific, where he had to make a water landing while being strafed by enemy fire. His landing gear had been damaged and he could not land on the field. He had radioed for help and a PT boat was sent to pick him up if he survived the water landing. He had not been able to bail out, as the prevailing wind would have carried him over the enemy lines. Except for a bump on his head, he made the landing safely, but the Corsair fighter plane he flew was lost to the sea. The PT boat had picked Red up quickly and a photographer on the PT boat had taken pictures of the water landing.

Red had also had two crash landings while in the States. Both crashes were because of faulty and damaged equipment on the planes. In Laguna Beach, he had made a belly landing because he was unable to get his wheels down, and once in Cherry Point, North Carolina, part of the cooling system had fallen out of the plane as he was coming in for a landing. He had made a "dead stick" landing in the smoking, damaged plane.

Red knew that he had been lucky to survive each of these crashes. Still, he felt that his service as a fighter pilot was easier, and probably safer, than was the fate of the ground troops who slugged it out in the hot, humid, insect-infested jungles and in cold muddy trenches in the European theater. Red's tour of duty each time he fought in the South Pacific took him to the tropical islands that had been invaded by the Japanese. His first tour of duty was as a day fighter pilot. The second time he was sent back to duty, he was a night fighter.

Red was in the Marine Air Core Reserves when the Korean conflict began, but because he was married and had two children, and because he was working as a fireman at a nearby military base, he was not called to active service. He had worked as a fireman for several years until he had been able to build up his accounting practice. He was tireless, working two jobs during the years after his return from the military.

Here, at his in-laws' home and next to his wife, Red felt happy and loved. He, like Harry and Henry, had put the wartime experiences behind him and had charged ahead with the business of living.

In the large back bedroom of the house, Ben and Elizabeth were also talking quietly about the day's events. They laughed as they remembered little Peggy's dancing with the Hula-Hoop. They also recounted the scare they had all had when Nancy disappeared and was later found in the woods with the great dog King, who had saved her from sure disaster.

The incident had turned out well for Nancy but not for King and had shaken everyone.

Ben and Liz also talked about Davy, Becka and Red's son, and Danny, Henry's son, eating watermelon and spitting the seeds at each other, while Sharon, Becka and Red's daughter, and Will's daughters, Darla and Rita, played badminton on the south lawn. Becka and Red seemed so happy together, as did Will and Edith, Henry and Helena, and Harry and Mikki.

Maggie Frances and Johnny seemed to really enjoy all the families and the commotion as well. Maggie Frances had been the main "mover and shaker" for the whole day. She had called everyone, arranged sleeping for family members, and planned food and games. She was in her element, and because she was a teacher, she was very capable of making things run smoothly.

Liz and Ben were proud of all their children and knew their special gifts, appreciating each one. They were both sad over the loss of the old dog, King, but were glad that he had given the last "full measure" of his life saving little Nancy. King had been an important member of the family and part of their lives for almost sixteen years, and they would really miss him.

Henry's wife, Helena, had been a real help in serving and planning the family event. She was always there for Liz and ready to help in any way she could. Helena, along with the rest of the family, felt the terror of the missing child and the loss of the old dog, King. She thanked God that the little girl was not hurt, and each time she thought of the incident, a cold shudder went up her spine.

Liz had been born into a family of seven children—the fifth child and one of five daughters. Elizabeth Eureka Sagraves was born in 1885. Her parents Sara and Green Sagraves were very young when they married. Sara was only fourteen and Green barely nineteen. Early in their married lives, they moved to a farm and opened a mercantile store. They also had a large farm with several acres of land, horses, a cow, and many chickens and rabbits.

Liz was no stranger to hard work. She had been assigned chores to do even as a small child. She later worked in the country store and graduated from Normal College to become a teacher in the small one-room school near her parents' home. Liz was a beautiful young woman, with blue-gray eyes, dark golden curly hair, a "peaches and cream" complexion, and an infectious laugh. She was one of those fortunate people who could almost always see the humor in everything.

Ben, who was a few months younger than Liz, was born in 1886 into a family of seven children. He was the youngest son and grew up on a large farm in Virginia. He was born Benjamin Ernest Young and had had the nickname of Hoss for as long as he could remember. He, too, was no stranger to work. All of his sisters and brothers worked hard to maintain the farm, cattle, horses, and a kitchen garden. Their father had been killed when Ben was but a boy, and as there was no insurance, their mother and all the children worked to keep food, clothing, and other necessities available for the immediate needs of the family.

Ben was a handsome man with a shock of black hair, fair skin, and steel blue eyes. He had a beautiful smile that showed even white teeth. He was well-built and very strong, and skilled in many areas. He had only attended fourth grade in public school but had continued to study through correspondence colleges, receiving certificates in electrical, mechanical, and mining engineering.

Liz and Ben's courtship had lasted over three years, so they were both in their late twenties when they married. They had moved to West Virginia where Ben had a job as the electrical supervisor of the mines in Chattaroy, West Virginia. It was a well-paying job, with a furnished home for Ben and family and a car provided. However, it was a dangerous position, as all mining jobs are. Liz continually begged Ben to look for other work. When he applied and was accepted at the American Rolling Mill Company—ARMCO—he moved with his family of six children to Ashland, Kentucky. They had made their home in this same house since then. They had reared all their children here and loved this old place. Hoss had made many improvements, and Liz had painted the inside walls, wallpapered and furnished the home with colorful and comfortable furniture. They were happy here and enjoying their later years together. They had no desire to leave, although Becka had often encouraged them to sell the old place and move to California. They had considered it and had spent several winters in Southern California but were always happy to return to the place they loved, the place that would always be home to them.

In truth, all the children loved this old home. It represented security and family love to each of them. They all enjoyed coming "home" although each had made homes of their own. Liz and Ben had been living examples of what a happy home should be, and each of their children had maintained long and enduring marriages. That didn't mean there were no trials, problems, tragedies, and sacrifices. There were many trials that could have ended in a broken home, but they did not. Each sibling had managed to work through his or her problems, whatever they might have been, and their families grew stronger for it. Ben and Liz were motivated and purposeful and communicated with each other and their children. They "worked things out" and managed to remain a close-knit, loving, and caring family. They had suffered tragedy in the loss of a dear son. They had pulled together and comforted and sustained each other.

Through the years, there had been many serious illnesses and accidents. Will, their oldest son, had almost been killed as a young boy when a large stone rolled down one of the steep mountains near the family's home in West Virginia. The stone had hit his head and almost severed his right ear. Liz had given him the proper first aid before the doctor arrived, and the doctor told her that she had indeed saved her son's life—and ear! He would have surely bled to death before the doctor could have arrived without her help.

Becka had been critically injured when she had accidentally fallen into a deep catch basin near the kitchen sink. She had nearly severed her right leg. Again, Liz administered the proper first aid and Becka's leg was saved and healed properly. There were other illnesses and accidents during the youthful years of the family, and all were handled with swift care and competence.

"Oh, Ben," Liz said quietly, "do you think we've done a good job with our kids?" Ben pulled her close, kissing her forehead. "Well," he drawled, "I guess we did the best we know how. I reckon that's all anybody can do." Liz felt his strong arms around her. She was tired and happy and a little sad.

She was sad because she knew that Becka and family and Harry and his family would soon be leaving—Harry to Florida and Becka back to California. Henry, Will, and Maggie and their families all lived in and around Ashland, and Liz and Ben saw them often. This was a great joy to them both. And Ben had a true comradeship with his sons. Maggie Frances, often called Sis, visited her parents at every opportunity. She was sensitive to her parents' needs as they grew older and often took them to the doctor or dentist. Will, too, visited his parents whenever he could, which was often. Henry and Helena and their children, Dan and Darrell, were frequent visitors as well.

Liz and Ben, or "Nanny and Hoss," as they were called by the grandchildren, were content with their lives and happy. Hoss was healthy and strong and kept the place in good order. Nanny loved to cook and grow flowers, and she did both with great pleasure. She had filled the house with pots of fresh flowers and had purchased new colorful towels and linens. For the celebration, she had helped Ben give new coats of fresh paint to the kitchen, hall, and front porch. Becka remarked with pleasure that she hadn't seen the place look so beautiful and inviting. Becka and Helena visited and laughed together about the antics of the boys and the events of the day. They loved each other as "sisters" and enjoyed being in each other's company.

Becka and Red

My Old Kentucky Home

CHAPTER 2

There Is a Place I Like to Go

There is a place I like to
go early in the day.
I go there every chance I get
when I can get away.
Not far it was, up a shady lane—
I could see my home, my birthplace,
sun glinting on roof and windowpane.

Betty Duncan-Goetz

*V*ERY EARLY in the morning, Becka slipped out of bed. She pulled on her jogging suit and put on a pair of tennis shoes. She wanted to take one last walk along the old trail to the area on the hill where she could see the river. The air was crisp and fresh; the sounds of birdsong could be heard, and the leaves rustled under her feet. She walked along the old familiar path, across the footbridge and up the hill to the spot where she could view the river and beyond. It was very early, and she had seen few people about. Lowering herself down on an old stump, she let her gaze take in the entire area. Slow-moving barges were making their way down the mighty Ohio River, on their lazy journey to the Mississippi River and beyond.

Becka remembered the time in 1942 before she had left for Washington DC. She and George, her neighbor and friend, had taken this walk. He had asked her to wait for him until he returned from the service. She had not promised but had said she would write to him. She also remembered walking this trail with Harry just before he left for the Navy. It had been a bittersweet time.

Now, in this early morning hour, she thought of all the changes that had happened in her life since then. Indeed, all their lives had changed so much, and so very many life-altering events had left their marks on them all.

She looked out across the wide, beautiful river and remembered the time in 1937 when Maggie Frances had brought her three younger siblings to this very spot in order to see the river during a great flood. She remembered seeing houses flooded on the banks and some floating down the river, with people trapped on roofs or clinging to pieces of wood or trees. The river was covering so much land and so many homes that Becka thought it looked more like the ocean than a river. It was the worst flooding in many, many years.

She was brought out of her musings when she heard the breaking of twigs and the rustle of leaves nearby. She looked down the trail to see Red coming toward her. His red-gold hair was ruffling in the breeze, and he wore a light jacket and jeans. He was a handsome man, six foot four, well-built, not heavy, and with long legs and arms.

"Hi, little Dolly," he said with a broad smile, "I thought I'd find you up here!"

"Hi, yourself!" answered Becka. "Come and join me!"

He put his arm around her, and they both settled down on the leaf-strewn ground. Becka pointed to the river and the barges. As Red followed her gaze, he remarked, "I wonder where they're going and what they're carrying."

"Well, I can't say what the cargo is, but I know where they're going. They're headed for the mighty Mississippi," Becka said with a smile.

"And we had better head back to the house before Liz serves breakfast without us!" said Red as he pulled Becka to her feet, and they moved slowly back down the trail.

"It's so beautiful here in the fall of the year. I love the changing leaves, the nip in the air, and the promise of winter," she mused aloud.

"Yes, I know," said Red, "but when the real winter arrives, you would be wishing you were in Southern California!"

"I know, I know," she said, "but I do often wonder if we were wise to move away. Then I think of the weather, the long winter of snow and ice, and the children making their way to school in that awful weather and I'm glad we live in California. But I do miss the folks and other aspects of Kentucky life," she said as she looked up at Red, squeezing his hand and smiling.

"Well," Red drawled in his Texas speech, "we had better get a move on and relish the aspect of your mom's great breakfasts!" He laughed and pulled Becka to a faster pace. She always had a difficult time keeping up with Red's long-legged stride and was puffing as they reached the house. The aroma of bacon and eggs filled the air, and both their mouths watered.

"Oh, there you are!" exclaimed Liz. "I hoped you'd get back soon. Your dad is hungry for his breakfast!"

"So are we, Mom," Becka said with a smile. "Just let me wash up and I'll be right in to help you get things together." She skipped off to the bathroom. Ben and Red sat down with cups of hot coffee. In a few minutes, they were served large portions of eggs, bacon, sausage, toast, and jams. Sharon and David, Becka and Red's children, were already finishing eating. When they were filled and satisfied, they asked to be excused, and hugging their Nanny, they ran outside to find their cousins, Danny and Darrell. Becka, Red, and her parents lingered over their coffee and talked about the trip to California. It would take approximately four or five days, and they had a full week before the children had to be back in school. They wanted to stop at several national parks on the way home.

Ben and Liz had driven to the West Coast several times, and Ben knew all the routes and could recite them from memory. He and Red went over the routes, deciding the best ways to get to the particular parks. The four of them also discussed the incident with little Nancy. They all agreed that Harry had been right in the way he'd handled Nancy. All the adults, including the police, thought it best to leave her alone until a later time, when her mother could take her to a doctor and a therapist as well. They had learned from the police that the man they arrested had a record of this kind of thing and had served time in prison. "I just can't understand how he could ever have been turned loose," Liz said with real anger in her voice.

"Neither can I!" said Becka angrily. The two men agreed with the women and voiced their hopes that the brute would be sent to prison for a long time. All four expressed their sadness, again, for the loss of King who had saved Nancy's life.

Although they never spoke of it to Ben or Liz, things were not going well with Red and Becka. Red was drinking heavily at times, and Becka worried about him and their relationship. She felt she knew why Red drank so much. He was under great stress working two jobs and trying to make financial progress. She had taken a job for the county as a social worker. It paid well and was helping the little family improve their circumstances. However, Red remained moody and stressed; he really didn't want her to work. He felt, somehow, that he was not "doing his job" of providing for the family. He was what Becka sometimes thought was "old-fashioned" in his belief that the wife and mother should stay home, not work.

On this point they disagreed. Becka had waited until the children were older and at school all day before she obtained a position at the local social welfare department. She had taken the civil service exam required and was in the top ten applicants. She was offered the job and gladly accepted. There was little or no public transportation from the area where they lived and it had been necessary on many occasions to borrow Red's car. Red didn't like being without his car and sometimes refused to let her borrow it. There were many arguments about this, and Becka convinced him that she needed her own means of transportation. The minister of her church was being relocated and sold her his 1951 Studebaker. It was in excellent condition, and Becka loved it, even though she said with the way it was made, you could never tell whether it was coming or going!

One Saturday afternoon, Becka was washing the car and looking sadly at the many nicks, scratches, and rusty places on its dusty blue paint color. Suddenly, a light bulb went off in her head! She drove to a local hardware store, bought a can of "Robin's Egg Blue" spray paint that she thought came pretty close to matching the car's color. She spent the next hour spraying each of the rusty nicks and scratches. When she finished, she stood back and looked at the car. It resembled a huge patchwork quilt! "It looks terrible," she said to herself.

Before Red could see it, she rushed back to the hardware store and bought every remaining can of Robin's Egg Blue paint they had and spray painted as much of the car as she could before she ran out. Three more trips to stores in and around Ventura and Oxnard and Becka finally finished up. It took twenty-seven cans and almost all afternoon to get the whole car painted, and it *still* looked a little spotty! Throughout the day, small groups of neighborhood children and a few adults gathered to watch, cheering when she finally finished! When Red came home and saw the car that evening, he just shook his head and laughed. Becka had the Studebaker for many years, teaching both her children how to drive using its stick shift. It was always called the "Spotted Blue Rocket" by the family and by Becka and Red's neighbors.

Becka loved her job as a social worker, and as she began to bring more money into the family, she begged Red to give up the job at the fire station and concentrate on building up his accounting practice. He finally agreed to do this, and things had settled down to a more normal family life.

Now, here in Kentucky with her parents, they were planning the trip home. It would probably be a long time before they made a return trip. In 1962, the children were into their teen years and often had too many school activities to be able to travel with their parents. Red and Becka had wanted this to be a special family vacation for all of them.

On this trip back to California, they would have time to visit several national parks and see interesting and beautiful areas of their great country. Both Sharon and Dave loved the parks and seeing the many sights along the way. For the most part they were good travelers, having fun and enjoying each other. Becka knew that soon they would not want to travel as much with Mom and Dad, because most teens preferred the company of their peers.

Zion in the Fall

Zion National Park

CHAPTER 3

Of Dreams and Reality

**Draw close to God, and He
will draw close to you.**

(James 4:8)

A FEW WEEKS before the reunion, Becka had had a very disturbing dream. It was unusual in the way dreams often came to her. In this dream, she saw much confusion, upheaval, swirling winds, herself crying and crying, and voices speaking that she did not recognize. She woke up feeling very uneasy and somewhat afraid.

She tried to forget the dream, but two nights later, it came back to her. She woke, crying out. Red was asleep next to her, and her cries woke him. He put his arms around her and said soothing things until she fell back to sleep. However, the next morning, Becka could not get the dream out of her mind. But, with so much to do, she was finally able to push it to the back of her mind, and now several weeks later, she had almost, but not quite, forgotten. So many times in her life she had had dreams that troubled her. So often, but not always, the dreams foretold events in her own life or in the life of someone in her family. Becka knew that there was absolutely nothing she could do to change or alter any coming events. As she had felt so many times in the past, she wondered why she had such dreams and why they came to her. She had been reluctant to talk to others about this, preferring to keep it to herself or at least keep it in the immediate family. Now that she was older, she rarely mentioned these dreams, even to her own family. When Red questioned her about her "nightmare," she just laughed and said it was probably due to the chili beans she had eaten the night before!

She had a sunny, optimistic nature, usually seeing the bright side of everything. Now here in Kentucky, she put all thoughts and anxieties in a small compartment in her mind and concentrated on the pleasure of the trip back to California. However, in the months to come, she would reflect on her dream as tragic national events unfolded.

That evening, after a wonderful dinner prepared by Liz, Becka and Sharon packed and made ready for the trip home the next day. Liz had loaded them up with homemade apple butter, candied yams, jellies, and cookies for the trip. She had arisen very early that morning and had golden fried chicken for them to take for a picnic on the first day's travel. It was a bittersweet parting for all of them. Becka and Liz could not keep back the tears. Everyone promised each other that they would write and call often and make a return trip soon.

The little family stopped at Cumberland Falls where they took advantage of the picnic area to enjoy the delightful lunch. The Cumberland area was very beautiful, filled with towering trees, mountain flowers, and a scenic river that was quite unique in its beauty. They spent the first night there in one of the cabins, getting up at midnight to hike down to the river falls in order to see a real "moon bow." The shimmering, ghostly moon bow thrilled the family, and Red was able to get a picture of it, although the photo did not do justice to the fantastic loveliness of the sight. Maggie's husband, Johnny, had told Red about his part in building the cabins and camping area around the Cumberland Falls. It had been when he was in the Civilian Conservation Corps (CCCs) and only nineteen years old. He and Maggie had been dating at that time, and he saw her when he came home on leaves. He took part in many such jobs during his time in the CCCs. Then when he was in his twenties, he had joined the Army.

After visiting Cumberland Falls, Becka's family drove on to Mammoth Cave in Kentucky and also visited Abe Lincoln's birthplace. From Kentucky, they traveled on west to the Grand Canyon, then on to Zion National Park and Bryce Canyon. The whole family, especially Red, fell in love with the national parks of Utah and Arizona. All in all, it was a wonderful family vacation trip home.

Red's accounting practice, Becka's work with the county welfare department, and school activities absorbed the family's time. But world events impacted the family and all the country. The "Cuban Missile Crisis" frightened the whole country with the fear of nuclear disaster. Becka took her children into Ventura and showed them the nearest fallout shelter to their schools so that if the country were attacked with nuclear missiles they would know where to find safety. The family stocked up on food and water and prayed with all their neighbors, their church families, and indeed the whole country that the "stand-off" would end peacefully. Both Dave and Sharon were very frightened as were all their friends. Some of the families built fallout shelters below ground. It was a tense and terrifying time.

Becka was thankful for her church and church family. The pastor of the little church was Elder Jack Evans. He and Red were good friends and spent many lunch hours together. He advised the family to pray and stay calm, if possible. Staying calm, when one felt so helpless, was hard to do.

That year, 1962, was a standout year for the whole world, as well as for the little family. Now living in a beautiful home in Ventura, Becka was very happy and the children, Dave, fourteen, and Sharon almost seventeen, were rapidly approaching young adulthood.

The Cuban missile crisis had been brought to an uneasy "peace" after several weeks of diplomatic maneuvers by Cuba, the USA, and Russia. The whole world breathed a collective sigh of relief, but many in America still did not feel "safe" and probably would never feel completely safe from the dreaded nuclear threat. The young president, John Kennedy, was intent on bringing the country back to normalcy and began a sweeping program of "putting a man on the moon and bringing him back to earth safely." This new and bold space program caught the imagination of the country, especially that of the younger Americans.

In February of 1962, Sharon had her seventeenth birthday. Becka planned a big party, inviting her many friends from high school and church. She baked a large cake with a spaceship on the top with the printed logo, "Friendship 17." This was in honor of her birthday but also about the upcoming space flight. Sharon's friends were all well-behaved, and there was no drinking or smoking at any of the gatherings she and her friends frequented. Red and Becka were both on hand for the birthday party, taking many pictures and enjoying the young folks.

Both Sharon and Dave were not allowed to attend any party or get-together without adult supervision. And this rule held true for the majority of those young people attending the birthday party.

Sharon was an excellent student and graduated with high marks that year. She was in many activities at school such as being the co-editor of the school paper, banner girl for the high school's marching band, violinist in the school orchestra and was voted "Girl of the Year" for 1961-62. She was in the first graduating class at Buena High School since it had just opened that year as the second high school in Ventura. The family lived only three blocks from Ventura College, where Sharon and Dave planned to attend after finishing high school.

Sharon dated several boys but had no one special in particular. She was still writing to a boy she had met in Ashland, Kentucky, but was not seriously thinking of becoming engaged or getting married. She had plans of her own and wanted to get an education that would help her reach her goals.

President Kennedy did not live to see the first man step foot on the Moon. Again, in the space of one year, the country was thrown into upheaval. The young President was assassinated in November 1963 while on a trip to Dallas, Texas. Becka was at work in her office when she got a call from a neighbor, who incidentally did not like the Kennedys. She told Becka with great glee in her voice that Kennedy had been shot. Becka's reaction was one of shock and disbelief. She told her caller that she didn't appreciate that kind of humor, and the neighbor told her to turn on the radio and listen to the news.

Becka hung up the telephone and quickly turned on the radio, and, of course, the first thing she heard was the dreadful account of the events that had taken place in Dallas. Quickly finishing her work for the day, she drove home in a daze. Dave had heard the news at his school, and promptly left, walking home in a state of shock. He arrived home shortly after Becka, and the two of them held each other in their despair. Dave, like his mother, admired the young handsome President and was deeply moved by his death. If the President of the United States could so easily be killed, who was safe from this type of madness?

Dave had actually met and photographed President Kennedy when the President had visited Point Mugu Naval Air Test Center near Oxnard, California, in May 1962. He had skipped school and ridden his bicycle the fourteen miles across the valley to the area where the President was to visit, and somehow (Becka could never figure out *how*), Dave was able to get into the receiving line and shook the President's hand, spoke to him, then sneaked out of the line and ran to the end of the line, shaking hands again with the President. Kennedy had looked at him and said, "I think we've met before, young man." He laughed. Dave laughed too, quickly left the receiving line, and rode his bike home.

Now, feeling a sense of despair, Dave was remembering that day in Oxnard. He was quickly leaving his childhood and entering a world of confusion and uncertainty. The Cuban crisis had jerked him out of his youth, and now this terrible event pushed him into a troubling world of upheaval and dismay.

In the coming days, the entire country experienced a drama unparalleled in modern history. It seemed the whole world was in mourning for the young President. His beautiful wife, Jackie, was an inspiration to many. She and her two small children conducted themselves with dignity and strength throughout that dark time. Becka had called her parents, who were experiencing the same sort of shock and disbelief. Liz and Ben both felt that the vice president, now President, would do a good job, but they were worried about the events taking place in Vietnam and the Middle East. Both her parents were worried about another war. Ben and Red discussed these things, hoping and praying that the U.S. would not become involved any further in this awful conflict that had already claimed the lives of young American servicemen and women as well as many wounded and some captured and imprisoned.

The new president, Lyndon Johnson, vowed to continue the space program, and in the summer of 1969, Neil Armstrong was the first man to step foot on the moon. The event galvanized the whole country and indeed the whole world. The Space Age had arrived! However spectacular and awesome as these events were, they did not stop the coming of the gruesome and terrible continuation of war in Vietnam. The USA had indeed become involved in this war, and many young people were drawn into the conflict.

In 1964, Red decided to invest in the restaurant business. He and three friends bought a franchise for Sizzler restaurants in the San

Diego area, and he moved his family there that year. Sharon was already attending college at San Diego State University and lived in a rented home for female students within walking distance of the college. Becka really didn't want to move; she liked her job and her home in Ventura. She wanted to keep it and rent it if possible. But Red wanted to sell. They found a nice smaller home in La Mesa and moved there.

Becka and Tawney

Becka and Wendy

Charlie

Dave, Reagan & Spike

Sauron

CHAPTER 4

All Things Come from God

**All things come from God, and
all things live by His power.**
(Romans 11:36)

IN 1966, Sharon graduated from college
and Dave was a graduate of Grossmont High
School. Dave had done well in high school,
even though he had been very unhappy leaving
Ventura, where he had many friends and was

involved in sports. However, he had made long and lasting friends at Grossmont High School and was fond of several of the teachers. He planned to enter Grossmont Jr. College in the fall.

Sharon had realized one of her goals, graduating from college, and was planning to continue in graduate school to get a teaching credential in Spanish. But romance had touched her life! She had met a handsome young lifeguard, fallen in love, and that summer they eloped to Las Vegas and got married. Both Red and Becka were understandably surprised and dismayed. However, they helped the young couple plan a wedding reception, and as a present, they paid for the first month's rent on an apartment in the area. They remained that first year in the apartment and then moved to St. Louis, Missouri, where Sharon's husband attended Washington University School of Medicine.

Dave had enrolled in the Community College and was busy with college classes and working part-time at the Sizzler with his dad. He found himself, listening to the war news, talking to friends who were either joining up or skipping off to Canada to avoid the draft. He debated in his own mind what course he should take. He knew his mom and dad wanted him to stay focused and in college. He listened to the war news and was in agreement with the reasons the U.S. was in this conflict in Viet Nam. He finally made up his mind and decided to join the Marines. Becka voiced her desire for him to stay in college, but if he was determined to join the military, to join the Navy or Coast Guard. She felt either of those services would be safer than the Marines. She too had been keeping up with war news and knew it was the Marines who were the fighting forces, along with the Army troops, in the jungles and ground war of Vietnam.

She and Red watched the news and dreaded the reports of wounded and killed young men and women. The reports were staggering. However, even with his mother's misgivings, Dave did join the Marines, and his dad, because he was a retired Marine Corps Officer, swore him in with Becka in attendance. Dave wanted to be a Marine Fighter Pilot as his dad had been during World War II, but his eyes were not keen enough for fighter planes. He became part of the ground forces, keeping the planes in top repair. After three years with his military service over, he returned to college.

The war went on for several years with the loss of many. It was a terrible experience for

America, not really winning or losing the war, but feeling, somehow, in limbo about the future of Vietnam and its people. The country was lost to Communism, in spite of the valiant efforts of the U.S. military forces. There was much controversy about the way the war was conducted. Red remarked that it seemed to him that the U.S. was trying to win the war with one hand tied behind its back. "Politics," he said, "are running things instead of the military." Becka and Red, as well as Liz and Ben hated war but understood the reasons for the conflict. The toll the war had taken on the country as a whole, however, was devastating and demoralizing. Anti-war riots took place throughout the country. Drugs were rampant, and most young people were affected in one way or another.

The 1970s were turbulent years for the country and for Red and Becka, also. The whole country was involved in the political battles going on in Washington. When President Johnson left the presidency, Richard Nixon was elected but became involved in political scandal, resulting in more political turmoil.

In 1970, Liz, who had been suffering with high blood pressure, and smothering spells at night, suddenly passed away. She slipped through "the veil" in December of that year. Becka flew home while Liz was in the hospital but did not arrive in time to be with her when she passed. Her brothers Will, Harry, and Henry, and sister Maggie, met her at the airport in Huntington, West Virginia. Will tenderly held Becka and tried to comfort her. Becka remembered again her dreams of several years ago. The loss of her mother was a terrible blow to her. Red flew to Kentucky to be with Becka for the funeral. It was many months before Becka began to feel "normal" again. She was teaching school, and the responsibilities of the classroom were helpful to her in taking her mind off her sorrow. Her church and dear friends at the church were a source of comfort to Becka. Her abiding faith helped her greatly, and the love of God was a strong, uplifting, and sustaining presence. She knew that her mother had only passed through the Veil and that she would see her again.

Becka was glad that Sis and Johnny were close enough to be a comfort to Hoss. Henry and Helena and their family were near and a comfort also. Hoss and Liz had been married for so long; it was a terrible tragedy for him. He missed her so very much, seeing her in everything he did. However, he stayed in the old home and managed his grief with dignity and grace.

The restaurant business was doing quite well during those turbulent years, and the income had enabled Becka and Red to buy a larger home in a beautiful new neighborhood. They had always wanted to do some traveling abroad and were able to take some wonderful trips, seeing many parts of the world and visiting many countries. Their restaurant was doing well, and Red had a great partner in Darrell Wade. He offered his help to Dave when he managed the restaurant while Red and Becka were away. Dave did an excellent job and liked doing it. Red and Becka felt good about leaving the restaurant in Dave's capable hands. Red also felt good about being able to take these trips with Becka. He knew it would be good for her.

In the summer of 1974, Red and Becka drove to Ashland and picked up Hoss for an extended automobile trip through the Southern states. They especially wanted to visit Florida, where Harry and his family lived. They drove all around the state. Ben seemed to thoroughly enjoy the trip, and he and Red laughed and talked about old times. One of the national parks they visited was the Everglades. On one of the days they were there, they had stopped and decided to take a wooden walkway to see a giant Mahogany tree. But it wasn't very long until Red and Hoss were slapping their legs and waving their arms over their heads! They both ran back to the car and slammed the doors. They said they were being eaten alive by mosquitoes! They hadn't affected Becka, though, as she had remembered to treat herself with anti-bug lotion. In spite of their bites, they all had a good laugh.

At times during the trip, Becka was quiet, remembering the time in 1966 when she had driven to Ashland and taken both her parents for an automobile trip around the country. They had visited many national parks and especially loved Yellowstone. They had had much fun and laughter together. Her mother had been feeling well then, enjoying the whole experience. Becka smiled to herself, remembering the time they had stopped at a small motel in the South. Becka had not managed to get to the clerk in time to pay for the room before her dad had gone into the motel office. When Ben came back to the car to help them unload, Liz asked him how much the room had cost. He shook his head and said, "Well, Ma, it cost forty-six dollars!" Becka had been paying for the rooms each night, and she had always told her dad that the cost was much less than it really was. She knew her parents didn't have a lot of money, so she was making up the difference.

That night, after Liz had showered and gotten into bed, she had asked Ben, "Daddy, did you lock that door?" He answered her, "Yes, Ma, I locked the door." In a few minutes, she asked him the same question again. Liz was partially deaf and had removed her hearing aid, so Ben raised his voice and said, "Yes, Ma, I locked it with a chain!" Liz was quiet for a few minutes, then said under her breath, "Well, I'll be dogged. Pay forty-six dollars for a room and have to chain the door shut!"

Becka and her parents had thoroughly enjoyed that motor trip. It had been good for all of them. Now as she traveled with Red and Ben, she missed her mother so very much. Yet she was happy that she and Red could have her dad with them and that he was having such a good time. Ben really loved Red and always called him "Colonel" for his retired rank in the Marine Corps Air Force. Ben was in excellent health and took care of himself fairly well. He had a helper who came in two or three times a week to clean, wash clothes, and do other needed household duties. Darla, Will's oldest daughter, spent time and helped Hoss when she could. Although he was grouchy at times, he nevertheless appreciated Darla's visits. Hoss was to live thirteen years after he lost Liz. He was ninety-six when he passed through the veil. The last two years of his life he lived with Maggie Frances and Johnny and their adopted son, John. He had had a mild stroke, and although he never lost speech or awareness, he was unable to care for himself.

One summer, before he had the stroke, Maggie Frances and her family had taken Hoss for a family reunion down in old Virginia. Hoss had many relatives there, and all loved to attend these large family "get-togethers." Hoss and two of his nephews, Claude and Roy, visited and laughed about the time the two boys had run away from home. They got as far as Kentucky and their Uncle Hoss's home—and had been put to work! Hoss had given them each a pick and shovel and had told them to "dig a basement." They had done a fair job and managed to have a lot of fun doing it, but they were glad to get back home!

Hoss loved seeing his younger sister Bessie and her very large family of ten children plus her grandchildren and great-grandchildren. Bessie loved Hoss and his family. She especially liked Liz, and the two women had long talks and enjoyed their visits together very much. Bessie was a handsome woman, strong and full of life, a hard worker, and as strong-willed as she was attractive. She liked crossword puzzles, word games, and excelled at all of these activities. She wrote poetry and was an inspiration to Becka. Bessie lived to be 106.

During the years after Liz passed away, Becka made several trips back to Kentucky and Virginia. Now she traveled alone, as Red was so tied up with the restaurant he often could not get away during the summer. She stayed with Ben to enable Maggie Frances to get away for a few weeks of vacation and rest. On one of the long drives from California to Kentucky, she was traveling late one night looking for a vacancy at a motel. As she drove past an on-ramp, she suddenly heard a loud firm voice on her Citizens Band receiver. "Just stay in that lane, little lady, as I'm going to slip by you on the right," and looking to her right, she saw an eighteen-wheeler roaring by in the next lane. She spoke to the driver over her C.B., and they began a conversation. He told her he was from upstate New York. He was married and had two children, a boy and a girl. He asked Becka what she was doing so far from home and driving so late at night. She explained that she was on her way to see her dad in Kentucky, had been driving for some time, and was unable to find a vacancy at a motel. He said he was pulling in at the next truck stop for gas and a cup of coffee. He asked Becka if she would like to have coffee, too. She was very tired, and a cup of coffee sounded good. "Yes, I would," she answered and followed the truck into the truck stop. The station was crowded with trucks and cars. She didn't need gas, so she parked by the restaurant. When she got out of the car, a good-looking young man, about David's age, walked up to her. "Hi," he said, "I'm Alan Cassalina. You must be Becka."

"Yes, I am, and I'm very tired and need that cup of coffee!" she said. They both smiled, and he escorted her into the large, noisy restaurant. Seating themselves, Alan ordered coffee for them both and asked Becka if she wanted a sandwich. She declined, and he ordered one for himself. They drank their coffee and talked for over an hour.

Finding the young man very interesting and easy to talk with, Becka enjoyed the chance meeting. He told her that some friends of his owned a nice motel not far away, and he called them to make her a reservation. They exchanged names, telephone numbers and addresses, and parted. She found the motel and had a good night's rest.

For the many years to follow, Becka and Alan kept up with each other and their families. Becka and Red visited Alan's home in upstate

New York, and Alan and his family visited Becka and Red in California. He met Sharon and David, and Becka and Red met Alan's family. The two families came to love each other as close and loving relatives. When Red and Becka visited Alan and his family, they were treated to a marvelous dinner, with a very Italian flavor. They ate on a spacious enclosed porch surrounded by beautiful large windows looking out onto a lovely flower-covered yard. While they were eating, many guests arrived, crowding in around the very large family table. They were all the cousins, aunts, and uncles of the family. All wanted to meet Red and Becka. It was a very delightful experience for all concerned!

When Alan and his family came to Becka and Red's home, Becka wanted to serve them a real California dinner. She made tamales, Mexican rice, and beans with tortilla chips and hot sauce for dip. Alan's family had never had any of this type of food before and did not know to remove the cornhusks from the tamales! Becka quickly realized she had made a large "boo boo" in her dinner plans! There was much laughter about the menu but not much eating by the Cassalina family. Becka was very sorry about the meal, but there wasn't time to serve anything else. The two families laughed about the "Mexican dinner" for years to come!

Dave Graduation Day 1966

Red in a submarine

*Becka and
Ray at Church*

Becka and Ray Cruising

*Red, Becka,
David and
Reagan 1982*

House in El Cajon

Joe and Sharon Cruising

Pumpkin Patch Great Grandkids

Ray and Becka in Front Yard

Ray and Becka in life jackets

Sharon, Red, Becka, Dave 1991

CHAPTER 5

Make a Joyful Noise

Make a joyful noise all ye lands!
(Psalm 100)

SHARON AND her husband, Lance, had two children, a girl and a boy, Laura and Luke. Becka delighted in both her grandchildren and babysat for Sharon as often as possible. She enjoyed her job as a teacher in the El Cajon School District. She loved teaching the young children in pre-kindergarten. Sometimes when it was possible, she took her own grandchildren to school with her. Little Laurie was a great singer and loved to teach the "little kids" new songs. At a holiday program, she taught and sang with the class. Laurie quickly learned to play the piano, and she and Sharon often played duets together. Luke liked the drums and made a lot of very loud, joyful "music" with them!

The year Laura was born, a lovely young Colombian girl came to live with Becka and Red. She was an exchange student from Cali, Colombia, and could speak English quite well, although with an accent. Red and Becka became her guardians, and she attended university while living with them. Carmen was a delightful addition to the family, since Sharon and Dave were both grown and living their own lives.

Carmen, who was eighteen, was a small young lady with long dark hair and eyes that twinkled when she talked. She had a beautiful smile and was intelligent and creative. She majored in art at the university and was a fine artist herself. She had never worked outside her home in Colombia, but she wanted to have a job in California. Becka took her over to a nice Mexican restaurant, and she applied for a job as a waitress. She fibbed a little and told the owners that she had had experience in Colombia. They believed her and hired her. She told Becka later that her first few days of working there had been near disastrous! But she kept her job and was able to pay most of her own way through college. After graduating from university, she met and married a good-looking young American man, and they made their home in the high California desert in Victorville.

Becka had arranged for them to be married in her and Red's home in El Cajon. It was a large, lovely home that lent itself well to hosting a wedding. Indeed, in the years to come, several weddings were held in their home. Red and Becka, as well as Sharon and Dave, loved Carmen as a dear member of their family. Becka welcomed Carmen and Mike's two boys, Mike, Jr. and Tommy, as special "grandsons" and Mike's daughter, Anya, as a special granddaughter. Carmen and Mike were quite successful in their different jobs, and just as successful as parents.

By the end of the 1970s, the country had settled down somewhat. The war in Viet Nam, though not forgotten, was not so much a "sore issue," but the experience of the war still often dominated political issues. Political battles between the two parties during the final years of the 1970s were hard fought and sometimes bitter. Becka and Red did not always agree on their votes, but they did not argue about them.

Ronald Reagan won with a large majority in 1980, and his confident, assured leadership was helpful in getting the country back to normalcy and a feeling of patriotism that had not been felt since World War II.

Since serving in the military during the 1970s, Dave had returned and taken advantage of the opportunity to finish college. Having taken real estate classes, he became an agent for a large real estate company in the San Diego area. Sharon, during the 1980s, was teaching at the elementary level. She loved teaching and planned to continue her career in education.

Becka and Carmen

Becka, Luke and Laura 1975

CHAPTER 6

Shadowed Veils between Life's Dark Storm Clouds

*T*HE FIRST years of the 1980s were difficult ones for Becka. In 1983, she lost her dear father, Hoss, and two years later, her much loved sister, Maggie Frances. It seemed to Becka that she was losing all her close family. Her oldest brother, Will, had also passed through the Veil during the late

1970s. Though she had experienced several disturbing dreams that foretold these events, she had tried to put them out of her mind but had not always been successful.

Both her sister's family and Will's family suffered sadness at the loss of their dear ones. Will, who had lung cancer, had lingered long and suffered much before passing. His wife, Edith, and daughters stayed close to Will, giving him much love and care. Edith did all she could to make him comfortable. Becka had visited Will several months before he passed and was impressed with the wonderful love and care he was receiving from his family. He had been in good spirits and laughed and joked with her, remarking that he would soon fix up his boat and take them all out for a spin on the river.

Maggie and her son, John, had driven her van to California to visit Becka and family. She had loved the trip, and she and John thoroughly enjoyed the San Diego area. As Becka remembered that visit, she felt sad but happy that Sis and John had been able to visit her and had enjoyed their visit so very much. Late in the 1960s, Harry and his family had driven out to California and visited with Becka's family. One of Harry's sons, James, spent several months with Red and Becka, attending Grossmont High School. During the early 1970s, Will, Hoss, and Henry had driven out to California for a visit. Henry and Helena had visited several times as well. They had enjoyed the visits and the sights. Red and Becka looked forward to all these visits and loved playing host and hostess to family members.

Red's grandmother, whom everyone called "Memo," was also able to visit the little family several times during the 1950s and 1960s. Red was so happy to have her come. She always rode the bus from Texas, as she did not like to fly. She kept the family laughing at her experiences on the bus. She related how she was attempting to enter the bus when a young man said, "Watch out for the little old lady!" She said, "I looked around for a little old lady and didn't see one!" She was a real "blast" when she went with the family to the beach to "catch" grunions, small fish, which come up on the sand during a high tide to spawn and lay eggs. She wore a pair of Red's jeans, went barefoot, and ran up and down the beach as though she were a kid, even though she was in her late seventies. She caught many grunions, brought them to the house, cleaned them, and fixed them for lunch. They were delicious! Red's Uncle Joyce, Memo's son, also came to visit and made a great hit with the whole family. He was fun and loved the children, who, of course, adored him.

After Becka and Red retired, they began to plan a long trip to the South Pacific, China, and Australia. Red wanted Becka to see the islands where he had been stationed and fought with the Marines against the Japanese during World War II. He wanted to see them again, himself, and to see how much they might have changed. He realized the islands would have rebounded from the devastation that they had suffered during the "Great War." The Island of Palau had been almost denuded of trees, animal life, and people. The natives of these islands, who could, had all left their once beautiful surroundings because of the destruction and their despair.

The U.S. had suffered also but more internally and mentally than physically, and though there were scars, they were harder to see. Red, who was an intelligent man, understood some of these deep emotions and feelings that the men who returned from their wartime experiences were feeling. He hoped, although he did not voice these hopes to Becka, the natives of these lovely tropical islands would be able to recover and rebound to something of their former lives. His own country had lifted itself out of the depressive Viet Nam era. Ronald Reagan was a charismatic president and inspired the whole nation to a renewal of pride in itself and its armed forces. Mr. Reagan encouraged family and church unity. A devout Christian, he prayed each day for strength and for his country. He had a delightful sense of humor and often made his listeners laugh. Red and Becka liked the new president and the way he was conducting policies in Washington.

Red had decided to retire and put the restaurant up for sale. He and Darrell had dissolved their partnership in the restaurants, and Red owned and operated only one. The restaurant sold for a good sum, and Becka decided, also, to retire from teaching. Red seemed much more relaxed and at ease. He rarely drank anymore, and when he did, it was just a social glass of wine with dinner. He had also stopped smoking.

Becka was delighted with this welcome change. She knew that Red would be in much better health. Both Becka and Red were active and enjoying work in the church. They helped establish a small mission in a little town near the border of Mexico. They drove to the mission about twice a month and donated time and funds to help the church get established. It was a rewarding and fulfilling experience for them both.

Teaching in school had been a satisfying job for Becka. She had continued her education at National University, graduating summa cum laude. She also took postgraduate studies, feeling well qualified as a teacher. But after so many years of teaching, she was looking forward to retirement. She also anticipated more time to write. She had always loved writing and was hoping to complete a novel, using her parents and family as the subjects.

After a few years as a realtor, Dave decided to get his teaching credential. He felt he would really like teaching and that he would, indeed, be doing something worthwhile. He especially liked teaching driver education, feeling that if he could manage to help young people realize the importance of safety and the dangers of driving recklessly, he would be successful. For Sharon and Lance, the marriage, after nineteen years, was not a happy one. With much soul searching, they finally decided to part. They divorced, and Sharon moved into a separate home. She continued to teach and became the principal of a local school, eventually going on to become the superintendent of three different school districts during her career.

During the 1980s, another young teenage girl came to make her home with Red and Becka. They sponsored her as guardians and considered her a very real part of the family. Elim was an intelligent, bright, and happy young girl. She loved living with Becka and Red and graduated from high school with honors. She had been unable to speak English when she arrived in El Cajon and moved into Becka and Red's home; however, she learned English very quickly and did extremely well in school. After graduating, she enrolled in a local community college. But soon, she met a handsome young Marine and she and Robert were married, with the ceremony taking place in Becka and Red's home. Many of Elim's relatives from Mexico attended the wedding, and Becka hosted a reception for the young couple. They were very happy together and had three handsome sons, Joseph, Eric, and Ezra. Red and Becka considered the three boys as "special grandsons."

By the late 1980s, Red and Becka were ready for that long-awaited trip to the South Pacific, China, and Australia. During the last fifteen or so years, they had been able to enjoy many trips, both domestically and abroad. One great trip was taken in 1976, the Centennial year. They had traveled to Europe, cruising the Mediterranean Sea, experiencing many countries and visiting numerous areas of ancient history. Both Becka and Red were enchanted with the cruise, the many islands, and interesting ports of call. The cruise ship, the *Golden Odyssey*, was almost new, and the crew did everything possible to make guests happy. And they were happy! The food was simply delectable. Becka gained five pounds! Red wouldn't say how much he gained, but he looked content and satisfied. Some of the people they met on the cruise became long-term friends, and they visited each other's homes and enjoyed holidays together. One of the pleasant things Red and Becka hosted was a Thanksgiving Day dinner at the Sizzler restaurant. The Sizzler was closed to the public on that holiday, so Red opened it for family and friends. Many close friends came, including some of the friends they had met on the cruise. Becka's cousin, Claude Ramsey's daughter Sandra and her family came with their little three-year-old son, and Becka's cousin Dan Davis and family came also. It was a very happy day, with lots of food, fun, and good spirits. During the last few years of the 1980s, Red and Becka hosted several Thanksgiving dinners for family and friends before Red sold the restaurant.

At one of these Thanksgiving dinners, an elderly gentleman came up to the door of the restaurant. Seeing the sign that it was closed but seeing the large group inside, he knocked on the door. Red opened the door and recognizing the old gentleman, invited him in and introduced him to the other guests. He joined the party of family and friends, and every Thanksgiving thereafter, he showed up for the "family" dinner.

Getting ready for the new trip was delightful fun as both Becka and Red wondered about ports of call. They were anticipating seeing new people and interesting sights. Red wondered how many of his old friends from his active duty days he would see. Thinking about the trip was especially exciting for Becka, who had never visited this part of the world.

The first week of the trip was to the Palau Islands where Red met a group of squadron buddies who had also been stationed there. He had hoped he would see some of his service friends but had no way of knowing who might be there. He was unable to get a list of those who would be on the trip. As it turned out, there were a few faces he recognized. There was much backslapping and remembering. The island had changed a great deal. The devastation of the jungles during the war had disappeared. The plants and animals had rebounded, and everything was lush with new growth and the sounds of animals everywhere. It was humid and very warm. The hotel where the squad was housed proved to be quite handsome, full of luxury, and had a very distinct island "feel." There were two swimming pools, walking trails, a small golf course, and many other attractions. But the main attraction for Red and Becka was the island itself. They toured the many water passages, seeing evidence of downed airplanes and other relics of the Great War. Becka and Red snorkeled the shallow waters along the beaches, observing the many species of tropical fish and marine life.

Food was a special treat, delicious and with a definite island flavor. There was fruit served at every meal: luscious papayas, mangoes, grapes, star fruit, dragon fruit, and many others. The weather was humid and warm even in January. In the evenings after dinner, the group enjoyed dancing to a great island band. The band delighted in playing songs they thought the flyers would like, putting their own type of island "swing" to every song.

The whole experience, the flavor, the new friends, and the enchantment of the islands filled the guests with feelings of satisfaction. When the time came for parting, it was with real regret. Red and Becka and the other members of the group exchanged addresses and so on, but all knew that they might never meet again. In truth, they did exchange holiday cards, but that, too, did not last.

Red and Becka prepared for the next leg of the journey: China. Red was very excited to be heading for China again. He was unsure of what he might find there that would be the same as when he had seen it last, almost thirty-five years before. Knowing of course, that things would be very different, he nevertheless was looking forward with anticipation. Becka also felt his excitement and was caught up in the adventure.

The weather in Beijing was very different from the islands they had just left. Think about the weather in Chicago in January, and one will understand the drastic change. Becka and Red donned their long underwear and heavy coats. They wore gloves and fur hats, soon looking like the natives. However, Red towered above everyone and was conscious of his height. Becka teased him about it, and they had some real laughs together.

They had made arrangements before the trip for a guide who spoke English. He arrived at the hotel promptly, and the excitement began. Becka could understand little of what Lin, the guide, said, but she and Red listened carefully and were able to understand a little more each day. Lin took them to the Great Wall, the Forbidden City, stage shows, monuments and places of great interest, especially to Red. The great city was amazing for its lack of automobiles. All Becka and Red could see were bicycles by the thousands, buses, and trucks. There were very few automobiles, and those were driven by Chinese government employees or dignitaries.

Red arranged for a taxi to take him, Becka, and the guide to various places. It was a true "nail-biting experience" driving through those bicycles, trucks, and buses. Red was amazed at the different look of the great city. Nowhere was there evidence of the profound poverty he had witnessed when he was stationed here during the war. He explained to Becka that during the war there was poverty, hunger, and homelessness. People roamed the streets, begging and ragged. Now, in this year of 1989, the change was dramatic. There could be seen high-rise apartment buildings everywhere. The people were dressed in warm clothing, and everyone seemed to have a bicycle. There were no beggars on the streets.

Their visit to Beijing lasted for nearly two weeks. During that time, they enjoyed the delicious food, the sights, the shopping, and the other guests at the beautiful Lido Hotel where they stayed. There was only one incident that troubled Red and Becka. One evening Becka forgot her reading glasses and returned to the room to retrieve them. She was quite surprised to find two men in the room. When she asked what they were doing there, they stammered and answered in broken English that they were changing the pictures. She looked at them and the room seemed not to be disturbed in any way. She told them she did not want them to change the pictures, that she and her husband liked them. The men nodded and picked up some form of equipment and left. When Becka returned to Red, she told him what she had seen. He nodded, and as soon as dinner was over, he returned to the room. Looking behind the pictures, he found a device, a "bug," for listening to what they were saying in the privacy of their hotel room. Red was quite angry, but he said nothing. Putting a finger to his lips, he whispered to Becka that he would play the TV and make no comments that would make the Chinese authorities suspect anything. He told Becka that he suspected the authorities were watching Lin, who had been involved in the recent student revolts at the university. The next time Lin was with them, they told him privately of the incident in the hotel room. Lin said he suspected this and wanted Red to pay him in "dollars" so that he could put them in the Bank of America. Red agreed and paid him when they could not be seen or heard by the Chinese agents. Both Red and Becka wished Lin good luck in his efforts to save money for his trip to the U.S. They told him he would be a welcome guest in their home and that they hoped he would be able to fulfill his goals. However, they never heard from Lin again.

The next leg of their journey took them to Japan. They landed in Tokyo. After getting settled in the hotel, they took a bus trip through the city. The city was clean and sparkling, its people friendly and accommodating. They visited temples and other places of interest. Everywhere they went, they were met with smiles and bows, and for some reason they could not understand, they were never allowed to pay any bus fare, but they never found out the reason. Red was treated as a visiting dignitary, and of course Becka, his wife, received the same treatment. They laughed and joked about it and took everything in stride.

Next came Australia and the Great Barrier Reef. In an amazing adventure aboard a large cruise ship, they traveled to the reef. They put on fins and snorkel masks and swam the waters of the utterly amazing and beautiful reef. Becka could not believe the abundance of sea life, from colorful coral to beautiful colored fish and crustaceans. The change in the weather from China to Australia was dramatic. January in Australia is summertime. The city of Sidney and surroundings was lovely, in full bloom, with flowers and flowering trees meeting the eye in all directions. Becka and Red took a train ride to inland parts of the area and visited other cities and the "bush," taking in the flavor of the culture, styles of dress, and different animal species. Red had visited the Australian continent during his tour of duty in the South Pacific, and this return trip was great pleasure for him.

All too soon, the six-week vacation trip was over, and it was time to return home. Becka kept a journal of the entire journey, and with Red's excellent photography, the whole trip was reviewed many times in future years. Again, on the air trip home, they visited Hawaii, where they stayed in the Royal Hawaiian Hotel, and for the few last days of their journey, they sat on the beach, ate late suppers, and enjoyed the glorious sunsets. Sadly, it was to be their last trip overseas together. Looking at the pictures many years later and reading the journal was bittersweet for Becka.

Bridge of Sighs, Venice 1976

South Pacific 1988

CHAPTER 7

She Said to Him, "Grow Old Along with Me."

She said to him, "Grow old along with me! The best is yet to be, the last of life, for which the first was made."
Robert Browning

*T*HE SIX years following their respective retirements were years of happiness for Becka and Red. They drove to Ashland several times and made several trips to local national parks, enjoying Zion, Bryce, and the Grand Canyon in the summer and winter as well as the Giant Redwoods in Northern California. Becka told her children later that those last six years with Red were the happiest they had ever had together. Red was relaxed and full of fun. He enjoyed dancing and visiting their many friends. He remarked that he had been a little afraid of retirement, thinking that he might become bored and restless. However, he was delighted to find that he did enjoy retirement and was especially happy being able to spend more time with Becka, enjoying her company, her laughter, and her love and spending time with Dave and Sharon. They both delighted in their grandchildren and Carmen's and Elim's children as well. Red loved children, and he was kind and loving with them.

Red also loved their pets. The dogs, Regan and Tawney, the cats, Spike and Wendy, plus the bird, Butch, all found this very large, gentle man a great pleasure to be with. He took the dogs for walks, played with them, and treated all the pets as "part of the family." Butch scolded everyone, especially the cats. He learned to whistle a tune that Red taught him, and he always whistled it when Red entered the room.

One of the very special pet members of the family was a big German shepherd dog that Dave had bought at a small pet shop near the Sizzler restaurant. He named the little fuzzy puppy, Sauron, after a character in a favorite book. The dog grew to be large and healthy, full of vim and vigor. He loved Dave and all the family. He felt he was their "protector" and guarded everyone at all times. Dave took him on mountain hiking and camping trips, taught him hand signals; the two were more like two brothers than dog and master.

Dave had a part-time job while he was attending college. It was a nighttime custodian's position, and he took Sauron along with him to work. He said he never felt even the tiniest bit afraid during this night job with Sauron there "on duty." Everyone in the family loved that Sauron was a very real member of the family, and when he passed away, it was as though a dear and loved family member had gone. The entire family mourned his loss. "Dogs just do not live long enough," Red said sadly, thinking of Sauron and Liz and Ben's dog, King.

In August 1994, Becka and Red traveled to Virginia for the Young family reunion. Harry and his family were planning to attend, as was Henry and family. However, Harry was not feeling well and they did not come. During the festivities, Becka received a telephone call. Harry had experienced a massive stroke and was in the hospital. Becka and Red left the reunion and traveled to Florida. They stayed with Mikki, visiting Harry in the hospital each day. His stroke was fatal, and he passed through the veil during the night. Becka and Red stayed with Mikki and comforted her as much as possible. Her children surrounded her with love and tenderness. Becka felt a deep sadness at the loss of this dear brother. She remembered the times as a little girl that she and Harry had shared with their brothers. They all had loved to climb trees, go fishing, ride bikes, and had had many adventures together. She had a close and dear relationship with her brothers. They had shared so many special times together.

The services held in Pensacola in Harry's honor were impressive and meaningful. An honor guard preceded the funeral procession to the cemetery. All traffic on the highways stopped and pulled off the road as the funeral procession passed. The honor guard led the procession into the gates. The mounted police dismounted and stood as the procession slowly passed.

The following year proved to be tragic for Becka, Sharon, and Dave. Red was not feeling well. Becka worried about him, but he insisted he was fine and he ate well. However, he was experiencing some vague chest pains. He consulted his doctor but was told "it's nothing to worry about," so he dismissed it altogether. It was a fatal mistake. On July 18, 1995, during a very hot spell, he had a heart attack and fell into the pool. Becka and Dave were home at the time and did not hear him cry out or hear the splash of the fall. Becka missed him, and after looking all over the house, she found him, floating facedown in the pool. He had little water in his lungs, and it was determined that he died from a heart attack while leaning over the pool to put chlorine in the water. Dave had pulled his dad out of the pool and started mouth-to-mouth resuscitation. In a terrible turn of fate, the home phone would not work and Becka had to call 911 from a neighbor's phone. It took the paramedics twenty long minutes to arrive. By that time, it was too late. In those twenty minutes, Dave had not stopped trying to revive his dad. When the paramedics finally arrived, they also tried to revive Red and decided to take him to the hospital in case there was a chance that he might live. Dave and his mother followed in Becka's car. But Red was gone. He had passed through the veil.

Becka's grief was so profound that she was completely numb and devastated for weeks. She had recurring dreams that haunted her. She was unable to sleep and lost weight. She was uninterested in life around her, avoided seeing friends and even her own children although they were very attentive and kind to her, staying with her at night and during the day as much as possible. Sharon took a week's leave from her job and stayed with Becka. She arranged for Carmen and Laura to stay as well. Even in his great grief, Dave spent as much time as possible, handling finances and helping to arrange "things." Laura, who loved her granddad dearly, calling him "Pop-Pop," was so glad that Red had been able to attend her wedding. She had been married in May of that year, and even then Red had not been feeling well, although he didn't say anything in order to not do anything to cause a disruption in the happy ceremony. He had come to Becka quietly during the bridal dinner party and told her he was going to go out and sit in the van. He slipped out quietly, and even though he felt sick, he stayed in order to take the flowers and gifts home in the roomy van.

The weeks and months after Red's death were a blur to Becka. She went through the days in a state of shock and weariness. "My life will never be happy again," she thought in despair. She could not eat, and her nights were filled with dreams of Red, struggling in the water and her feelings of helplessness. She often awoke crying, her body shaking with chills. Several weeks before Red's death, she had had a disturbing dream. In the dream she saw herself, as from a distance. She was alone and crying, crying. Then she awoke and could not get the dream out of her mind. But over time, she was finally able put the loss of Red in a back "room" of her brain and went on with her life. At times, though, she would remember the dream, feeling the loss and pain with renewed despair.

Zion National Park: The Arch

Zion National Park: Checkerboard Mesa

CHAPTER 8

For Now We See through a Glass Darkly

**For now we see through a glass, darkly; but
then face to face: now I know in part; but
then shall I know even as also I am known.**
(1 Corinthians 13:12)

IX MONTHS after Red passed
through the Veil, one of Becka's very special

friends called her. "Hi, Becka," Bailey said. "You are going on a cruise with me! Now don't say no! Just listen. It's a cruise through the Panama Canal on the very special cruise ship, the Radisson Diamond Seven Seas. It is an absolutely gorgeous ship, holding only 350 guests with a crew of 350!"

She continued before Becka could speak, "There will be fifty CEOs and their wives aboard. They practically have the whole ship reserved, so all the other guests will receive large discounts."

"Oh, Bailey," Becka said, "I don't think I can go. I just don't feel like taking a cruise." She felt she could never travel again, not without Red.

"Look, honey," Bailey said with conviction in her voice, "You can do it. We can go together, and it will be fun and interesting. You think about it. You have time. Just think about it before you refuse. You can afford it, and it's going to be a fantastic adventure. You told me once you've always wanted to traverse the Canal, and now is the opportunity of a lifetime! Just give it some thought, please. I'd love to have you as a traveling companion."

Becka promised to think about it. Bailey was ten years her senior. She had traveled all over the world with her husband, Frank, who was a public speaker. Bailey spoke five languages and was an interesting and fascinating friend. Becka loved and respected her. She knew that traveling with Bailey would be interesting and never dull. Bailey was an accomplished pianist and organist and had been a concert soloist in her youth. Becka talked it over with Sharon and Dave. Both her children felt she should go and that it would be good for her.

Six weeks later, the two women left for the airport and flew to San Juan, Puerto Rico. The next day, after a long bus ride, they boarded the ship and the adventure began. Becka, who had been on other beautiful cruise ships, could not believe the beauty and grand design of this ship. Every luxury that could be imagined was present. The elevators seemed trimmed with gold, and the staterooms left nothing to be desired. The dinners were fabulous and the other guests delightful.

Becka enjoyed herself in spite of her grief. She had moments of deep sadness but was able to overcome them and look forward to the adventures of the voyage. As her friend Bailey had promised, it was a wonderful voyage, full of surprises and delight. The ship visited many areas in the Caribbean and the Virgin Islands. Bailey conversed with any and all the natives. She was totally at home with the passengers as well as the crew. The two women were invited to share the Captain's table, and in the evening, Becka was asked to dance with several of the handsome officers.

Several months after returning home from the cruise, and ten months after losing Red, Becka had one of her "dreams." In this dream, she entered a large gymnasium, and looking across the wide gym floor, she saw Red sitting on a bench. He was dressed in shorts and seemed to be watching Becka as she made her way across the floor to his side. In the dream, she was very angry. She stood in front of Red, her hands on her hips, and looking at him with blazing eyes, she said, "What's the matter with you? Why don't you come home?"

Red looked up at her, shook his head, and got to his feet. After looking a long time at Becka, he walked away from her down a long dark hall adjoining the gym. Becka watched him go, her anger mounting. She marched out of the gym and climbed into her brand new car. "I'm glad he's not coming home right now. He wouldn't like it because I bought this new car," she thought to herself. Then she woke from the dream, feeling shaken and sad. The very next night, she had almost the same dream. She was again in the gymnasium. She couldn't understand Red's going there. He really didn't like working out at a gym. This time in her dream, she saw Red sitting in the same spot. He watched her cross the floor, and as she approached him, he stood.

"Darling," she said, with tears streaming down her face, "why don't you come home? Are you mad at me?" Red reached for her, and holding her in his arms, he said, "Dolly, don't you know that I cannot come home, ever again?" He whispered the last part of the sentence into her hair. Becka woke. Her pillow was wet with tears, and she was shaking as if from a deep chill.

The next day, Becka went into the large walk-in closet. She had gone into the closet many times, taking Red's clothes into her arms and smelling them, feeling him close, as if he were in the room with her. Now she took down the clothes, gently removed the hangers, and folded each shirt and jacket carefully, putting them in a box for charity. The task took her most of the day. She cleaned out the closet and the dresser drawers and put all of his things tenderly away. The dream had given her some closure. She realized that her subconscious mind had not released him. Unconsciously, she had been expecting him home, and although her conscious mind knew he was gone, still, she had not been able to accept it.

Now, she realized that her great sorrow had caused her to try to hang on to Red, even in death. She talked to members of the priesthood in her church and was able to receive much comfort. Her good friend, Joyce, and many others from her church surrounded her with love and understanding care. Gradually, Becka was able to accept the loss and the pain. Though it was never gone, it did grow less intense.

Panama Sunset

Red 1945

CHAPTER 9

There's an Old, Old Path

**There's an Old, Old Path
Where the sun shines thro' Life's dark
storm clouds in its home of blue.**
Vida E. Smith

*T*HE DAYS rolled on, one day telescoping into another. Becka tried to keep up with church and other similar activities. She had felt the call of the church to accept an office in the priesthood, and although feeling unqualified and hesitant to accept, she nevertheless did accept the "calling" and tried her best to fulfill her responsibilities.

This was a blessing for her. It gave her opportunities to reach out to others, and to forget her own problems. Being a part of her church and church activities meant a great deal to Becka, and she felt that her service, small as it was, seemed to be helpful.

Sharon and Dave felt the loss of their father in many ways. Both of them renewed their efforts in their separate jobs. Sharon had been on the point of receiving her Doctorate in Educational Leadership just before Red's death. She continued with her studies and graduated at the top of her class, receiving her Ed.D. That summer, she applied for a job as Assistant Superintendant in the Ojai Unified School District near Santa Barbara and was offered the position. She went on, in later years, to become Superintendent in three California school districts, one in Camarillo, one in Hermosa Beach, and one in San Diego.

Dave also discovered he loved teaching and went on to take a position as a high school teacher in science and history. Both Sharon and Dave loved their jobs. Becka was so happy for them. She loved teaching and had taught in the schools for twenty-one years as a pre-kindergarten teacher. It was during the time when Red owned and operated the restaurant that she had enjoyed the teaching position. The little ones were very dear to her, and she found it rewarding and full of fun and excitement.

During this time, a dream Becka had had seven years after her mother's passing often came to her mind. In this dream, she saw herself walking into the little Ventura church. The Pastor, Roy Ash, was speaking. He nodded his head as though he wanted her to sit on the right side of the church. After she was seated, she looked around and saw her mother sitting and smiling at her! She could not believe her eyes! Liz motioned for her to come sit with her. Becka did so and tried to speak to Liz; however, Liz put her finger to her lips and they both sat quietly until the close of the service. In the dream, Becka saw everyone in color, how they were dressed and how they looked. Her mother was dressed in a familiar blue suit, and her hair was in perfect shape, as though she had just left the beauty parlor. As they left the church after the service, everyone shook hands and some hugged Liz, remarking how good she looked. In the dream, Becka was very perplexed. She knew her mother was gone. Was she herself dead, she wondered?

Liz walked over to Becka and taking her hand, she asked her quietly why she was so troubled. Becka said, "Mom, how can you be here? You're gone! I don't understand." Liz shook her head and said, "I'm here because you wanted me to come. I'm just waiting." "What are you waiting for?" asked Becka. "I am waiting for your dad," she said simply. Becka woke up and still felt the presence of her mother. This dream had given her much comfort, and instead of crying, as she usually did with these kinds of dreams, she felt happy and lighthearted. She knew her mother was happy and content in her "dwelling place."

Continuing her social activities, Becka gradually began to do more things that involved others outside her own social circles. During a meeting of retired teachers, she met a nice man who invited her to go out to dinner with him. She accepted his invitation and enjoyed the evening. However, she felt a sense of unease and awkwardness during the evening and refused other invitations. Sharon and Dave encouraged her to "do more socializing," but she hesitated. "I'm just too old! I'm past all that!" she would say to them. "No, you are not!"

Sharon told her. "Dad wouldn't want you to just stay home and feel sorry for yourself." Becka did not feel sorry for herself, she thought. I just feel sad and lonely, and I miss Red so very much.

In the following months, she did accept other invitations to dances, picnics, church affairs and so on, but she really did not enjoy them and was not impressed with the men who asked her out. Oh, they were nice enough; they treated her with respect, and at times she had found herself enjoying their company, but she felt no real feelings for any of them.

In April 1999, some dear friends invited her to dinner. She explained to her friend Jeannie that she did not drive at night as the lights of other cars bothered her. Jeannie said her husband, Darrell, would come and pick her up. Becka asked Jeannie who else would be present at the dinner party. Jeannie hesitated then told Becka that her son's father-in-law would be there. "Oh," said Becka, "are you trying to play cupid?"

Jeannie laughed and said that since her son's father-in-law was alone, having lost his wife a year earlier, she just thought that Becka and Ray would both enjoy a good dinner with good friends.

Darrell picked Becka up that evening, and they drove over to Christopher's home where Jeannie and Darrell were "house-sitting" for their son and daughter-in-law. It was a lovely home, and the dinner was delicious. During the evening, the four talked, laughed, and enjoyed each other's company. When Jeannie served ice cream in the living room after dinner, Ray wanted to help. But his "helping" resulted in his spilling the ice cream on Becka's slacks! He was so embarrassed that he tried to wipe it off, only making the stain worse. Becka was amused and told Ray not to worry about it. She had liked Ray from the first and had really enjoyed getting to know him. When it was time to go home, Becka hugged Jeannie and Darrell, telling them that the dinner and the evening were great. Ray stood over to one side and, looking at Becka with a grin, said, "Don't I get a hug too?" Becka smiled and walked over and gave him a hug. "Can I have your phone number?" he asked. Becka gave it to him. She had a feeling at that moment that Ray would be a nice man to know. As she was getting into the car, Jeanie asked her if Ray had asked for her phone number. Becka grinned and nodded. Jeanie grinned back.

As Becka was getting into bed that night, the telephone rang. "That's Ray," she thought as she picked up the phone. It was. Becka laughed and told him she expected him to call her before she retired for the night. "I had a good time tonight," he said. "I hope we can see each other again soon." "I think that would be fun," said Becka.

Becka and her longtime friend, Billie Merrill, had planned a Mississippi River cruise that also included taking in the Kentucky Derby. The cruise was planned to start the next week. Ray looked up all the information about the Derby and gave Becka a copy of the names of all the horses and their riders. He also wrote a very sweet poem for Becka before she left for the cruise. Becka was impressed and used the information about the horses and jockeys to bet on each race. To her amazement, she won every race she bet on! She really "bet the jockeys" and not the horses. She won enough money on the races that her whole trip was paid for! When she returned home, she called Ray and told him the amazing news. He just laughed and said, "Let's go out to dinner." And so it began.

Becka & Ray
at Christmas

Niagara Falls

Becka on the Cruise

Becka on Drums

Musicians Ray and Becka

Ray on the Autoharp

EPILOGUE

ECKA SAT alone on the patio with the sun warm on her shoulders. She loved sitting in the swing, looking at the blue sky, the tall trees, and the sweeping view of the valley, listening to the bird calls and generally doing nothing but letting her mind wander back over the many years of her life. Her thoughts ranged from her early youth to now, her senior years.

She and Raymond were very happy together. Their marriage had been joyful and full of fun. The wedding had taken place in the home that she now shared with Ray. Dave had "given her away," and Ray II had been best man. All of both families had attended, with Ray's two small grandchildren serving as flower girl and ring bearer. Sharon, who held the office of Priest in the Community of Christ Church, performed the ceremony. Sharon was beautiful in a pale pink outfit, and Becka wore a long gown with a white lace hat. Ray told her later that she was the most beautiful lady in the house. Becka smiled and said she was happy he thought so, but she knew he was a little biased! Carmen had acted as Becka's attendant and had arranged for a friend to play the harp during the ceremony and at the reception. Becka's good friend Marilyn had sung a beautiful song. Her friend Shirley played the organ for Marilyn, and they sounded wonderful together even though they had been unable to practice beforehand. The wedding went well, and they left that night on their honeymoon to Niagara Falls.

Two years later, Sharon married Joe, a handsome and wonderful man who was a school superintendent near the district where Sharon was superintendent. She had been dating him for several years. They were married on Becka's patio, with Becka performing the ceremony. Becka was an ordained Elder in the Community of Christ Church, and both Sharon and Joe wanted her to preside at the ceremony. It was summer, and everyone was in Hawaiian dress. Sharon and Joe had bought a "time share" in Hawaii, and that is where they planned to honeymoon. The ceremony was very happy and colorful, with Laura's two children, Conor and Cade, acting as ring bearers. Becka was delighted to perform the ceremony, remembering her own wedding to Ray two years earlier. She and Ray, with David's help, hosted a fun and laughter-filled reception after the wedding. Carmen helped with the reception, adding her special touches to everything.

Becka and Ray shared a cruise with Sharon and Joe. It was a fun and happy experience. The fall weather was great. The trip down the Pacific with interesting ports-of-call in Mexico was very educational. The food was delectable and there was a great band for dancing. There were swimming pools and all the amenities needed for a fabulous vacation. They all agreed that another cruise in the near future was a <u>must</u>!

Becka and Ray had love, mutual respect, compatibility, and joy in their marriage. They had both had their share of illnesses, and each had been caring and loving during those trying times. Becka had become almost blind when it came to reading or doing any kind of close work. The doctors said she had macular degeneration, and although she would never be completely blind, she would be unable to do anything that required detailed vision and she would not be able to drive. Not driving was the hardest part. She had not been able to drive for the past several years. Ray was patient and willing to do all the driving. So far, Ray had been in excellent health, with only one spell in hospital with a bad kidney. He recovered in record time and seemed to get along without the kidney just fine, thank the good Lord!

They led a fulfilling life and were busy with many activities, traveling and enjoying their respective children, grandchildren, and great-grandchildren. They expected to celebrate their fifteenth anniversary at the end of the summer. Becka took classes in the use of the computer with a teacher at the Blind Center. She had met many friends at the Center and also took other classes there. Ray was a volunteer and was beloved by all of the ladies for his helpful, kind ways.

Becka had lived through the Great Depression, World War II, the Korean Conflict, the death of a young president, his brother, and Martin Luther King, Jr. as well as the turmoil of Viet Nam, and the deaths of all of her nuclear family. Henry Robert and his wife, Helen, the last of her nuclear family had passed away within months of each other. Becka felt the loss terribly and mourned again all of those who had passed through the Veil.

Will's three girls, Darla, Rita, and Billreka Renee, along with Maggie and Johnny's son, John, were a comfort to talk to and visit with, especially by telephone, keeping each other up on various happenings in Ashland, Kentucky. Steve, Harry's son, visited Becka and Ray in California and promised a return visit soon.

Becka had been present at the marriages of her children and grandchildren, the marriages of her adopted daughters, and the heartbreaking death of Red. Then she had met Raymond, and the result was a late in life marriage filled with joy and love. The terrible tragedy of 9/11 and the resulting war in Iraq had taken a toll on all of them as had the downturn of the economy. However, they all were weathering these enormous problems with dignity and stability.

Looking up at the wide expanse of blue sky, the call of birdsong, the view of the city, and the valley below, Becka's heart filled with gratitude. Her prayer was simple:

"Thank you, Heavenly Father, for all your blessings to me and my loved ones. Thank you for the many times you have lifted me up, held my hand, and given me comfort. Even now, I feel your loving arms around me and feel the presence of those who have passed through the Veil." As Beulah, an old friend of long ago wisely stated, "the Veil is mighty thin betwixt us and those we love. We have not lost them . . . they are always there when we remember."

And we remember.

DEDICATION

*T*HIS BOOK is dedicated to all those who are now shrouded by the Veil. It is also dedicated to those present and well loved. Thanks to my children and especially to my husband. Their help and kindness cannot be measured. I wish also to thank the wonderful folks at the Center for the Blind. Through them, I was able to learn computer skills and so much more. May God bless you all! Betty L. Duncan-Goetz

ACKNOWLEDGEMENTS

*T*HIS BOOK is a memoir, dedicated to family and friends. It also contains fictional stories for reader interest. The account of Little Nancy and the near disaster was based on an actual event that happened in San Diego near the author's home.

Thanks for the memories!

The author may be contacted at www.rblg337@ yahoo.com